Ledger

MW00426769

37

38

39

40

25

24

23

22

18

19

20

21

6

5

4

3

C D E F

A. Name the notes.

1. C ___ ___ ___   2. ___ ___ ___ ___

3. ___ ___ ___ ___   4. ___ ___ ___ ___

B. Unscramble the letters to spell a state.   O A I W

Clue: This state is famous for corn.

___ ___ ___ ___ ___

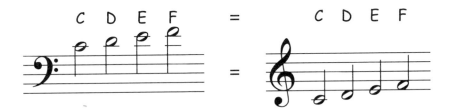

A. Name the bass clef notes.

B. Match the 𝄢 ledger lines to the notes that sound the same in the 𝄞 by writing the correct number in the leaf.

4

A. Draw lines matching each group of letters to the correct notes on the staff.

B. Shade the correct keys on the keyboards next to each note set.

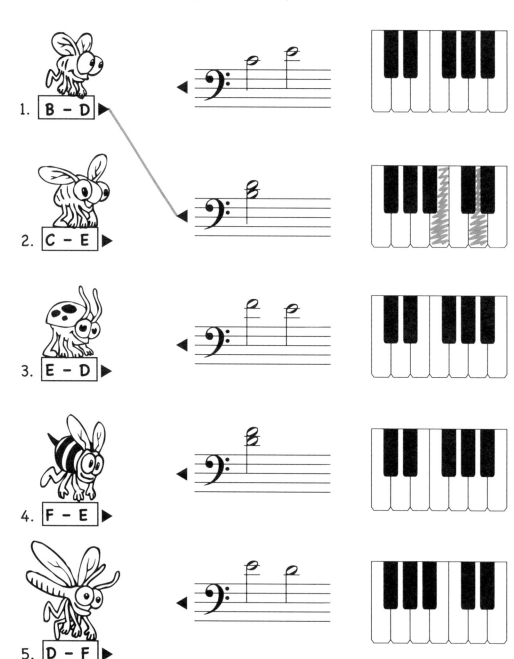

1. B – D

2. C – E

3. E – D

4. F – E

5. D – F

A. Name the notes.

B. Write the numbered notes on the staff in the correct place on the keyboard. There may be two numbers on some keys.

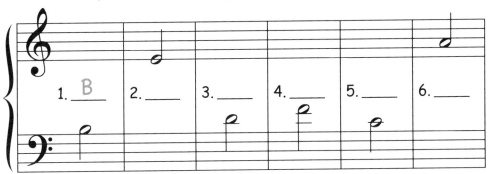

1. _B_ 2. ____ 3. ____ 4. ____ 5. ____ 6. ____

7. ____ 8. ____ 9. ____ 10. ____ 11. ____ 12. ____

Middle C

C   B   A   G

A. Name the notes.

1. C __ __ __ __   2. __ __ __ __

3. __ __ __ __   4. __ __ __ __

B. Unscramble the letters to spell a state.

Clue: This state is home of the Golden Gate Bridge.

__ __ __ __ __ __ __ __ __ __

N   O   A   A   I   F   C   R   I   L

A. Name the treble clef notes.

B. Match the 𝄞 ledger lines to the notes that sound the same in the 𝄢 by writing the correct number on the caterpillar.

1. C

2. _____

3. _____

4. _____

8

A. Draw lines matching each group of letters to the correct notes on the staff.

B. Shade the correct keys on the keyboards next to each note set.

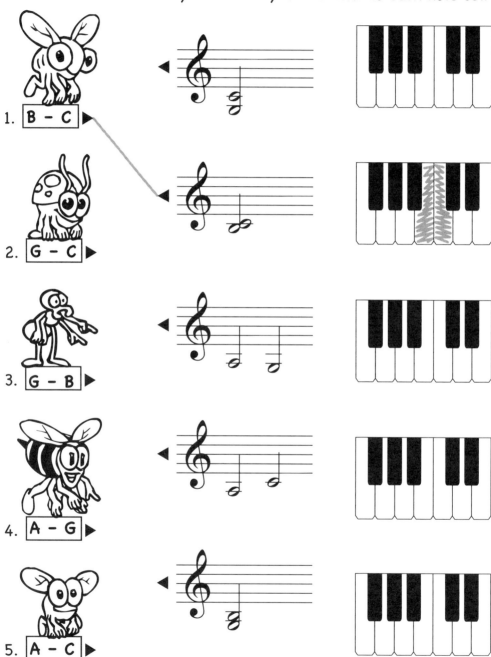

1. B – C

2. G – C

3. G – B

4. A – G

5. A – C

KP28

A. Name the notes.

B. Write the numbered notes on the staff in the correct place on the keyboard. There may be two numbers on some keys.

1. _C_   2. ____   3. ____   4. ____   5. ____   6. ____

7. ____   8. ____   9. ____   10. ____   11. ____   12. ____

Middle C

A. Write the letter names of the given notes to spell words.

1. E D G E   2. _ _ _ _   3. _ _ _

4. _ _ _ _ _ _ _   5. _ _ _ _ _ _

B. On the following pages, unscramble
the letters to spell states.

Clue: This state is famous for Niagara Falls.

___ ___ ___   ___ ___ ___ ___

R   K   O   N   Y
   E   W

Clue: This state is famous for its skiing.

Matching

A. Draw lines matching each group of letters to the correct notes on the staff.

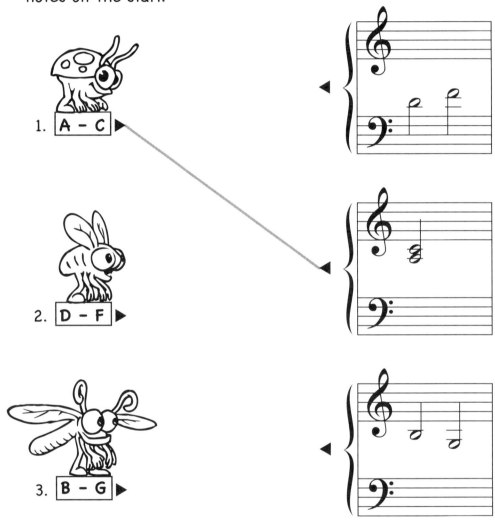

B. On the following pages, unscramble the letters to spell states.

Clue: This state is famous for the great lakes.

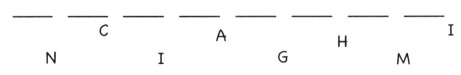

4. C – F ▶

5. B – E ▶

6. B – C ▶

Clue: This state is famous for New Orleans jazz and Mardi Gras.

___ ___ ___ ___ ___ ___ ___ ___ ___

I L U A A S O N I

◆ Remember that **C** is on the second line above the treble staff. You can figure out the other notes by steps and skips if you remember **C**.

A. Draw three C's.

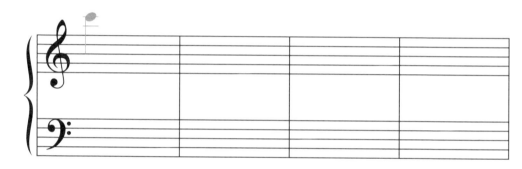

B. Name the notes.

A. Draw lines matching each group of letters to the correct notes on the staff.

B. Shade the correct keys on the keyboards next to each note set.

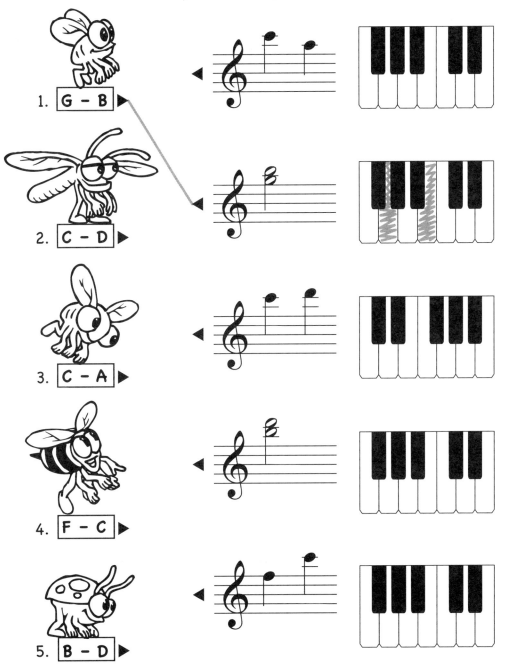

A. Name the notes.

B. Write the numbered notes on the staff in the correct place
on the keyboard. There may be two numbers on some keys.

1. _A_ 2. ____ 3. ____ 4. ____ 5. ____ 6. ____

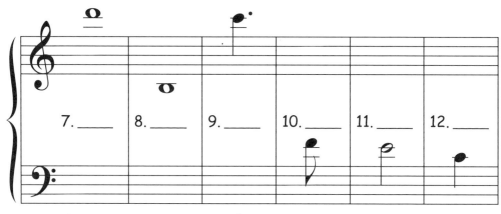

7. ____ 8. ____ 9. ____ 10. ____ 11. ____ 12. ____

Middle C

Coloring Note Page

18

E D C B

◆ Remember that **C** is on the second line below the bass staff. You can figure out the other notes by steps and skips if you remember **C**.

A. Draw three C's.

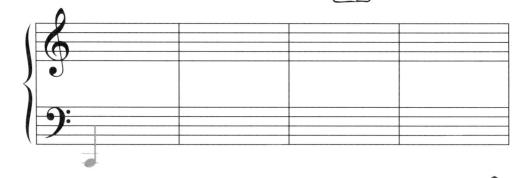

B. Name the notes.

1. ___ ___ ___ ___   2. ___ ___ ___ ___

A. Draw lines matching each group of letters to the correct notes on the staff.

B. Shade the correct keys on the keyboard next to each note set.

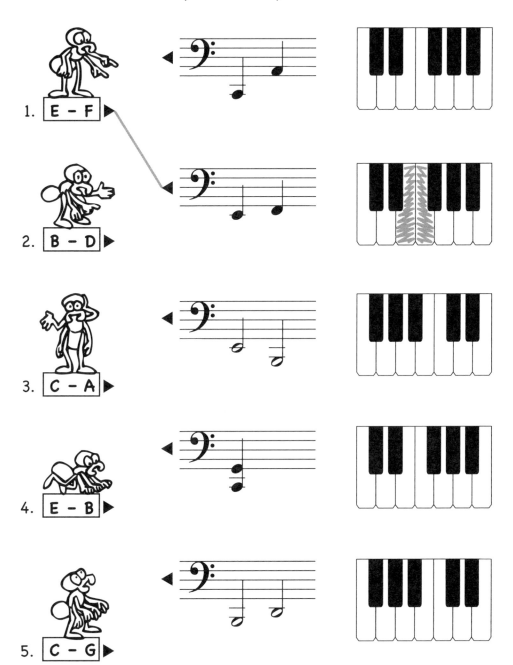

20

A. Name the notes.

1. D 2. ___ 3. ___ 4. ___ 5. ___ 6. ___

7. ___ 8. ___ 9. ___ 10. ___ 11. ___ 12. ___

B. Write the numbered notes on the staff in the correct place on the keyboard. There may be two numbers on some keys.

Middle C

Coloring Note Page

Color the: G's red   D's orange   F's brown
E's blue   B's yellow   A's green
C's purple

KP28

A. Name the notes to spell words.

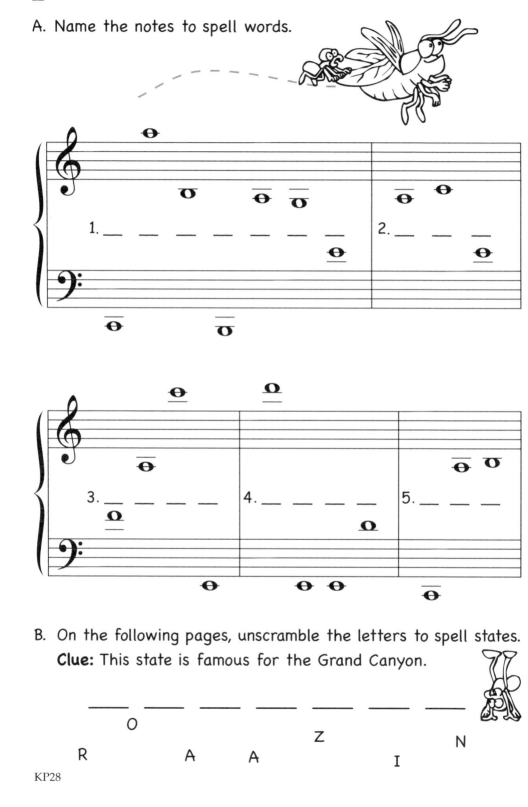

B. On the following pages, unscramble the letters to spell states.
Clue: This state is famous for the Grand Canyon.

Clue: This state is famous for Glacier National Park.

___ ___ ___ ___ ___ ___ ___

     A

                               N

A   M   O   N   T

_____

can name all of the ledger line notes on the staff
with ease!

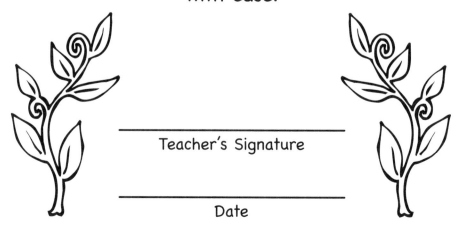

Teacher's Signature

Date